Biennial Report to Congress on Improving Industrial Security

U.S. Department of Defense

July 30, 2011

Preparation of this report/study cost the Department of Defense a total of approximately $6,451 for the 2011 Fiscal Year.
Generated on 2011Jul05 1506 RefID: 5-A1AA90A

Biennial Report to Congress on
Improving Industrial Security

This report complies with Section 845 of the National Defense Authorization Act (NDAA) for fiscal year 2009 (Public Law 110-417), which requires the Secretary of Defense to report biennially to the congressional defense committees on expenditures and activities of the Department of Defense (DoD) in carrying out the requirements of this section (i.e., Defense Industrial Security).

Unless otherwise stated, all information contained in this report covers the reporting period of fiscal year 2009 through fiscal year 2010.

Topic I: The workforce responsible for carrying out the requirements of this section, including the number and experience of such workforce; training in the performance of industrial security functions; performance metrics; and resulting assessment of overall quality.

The below chart reflects DSS planned workforce for fiscal years 2009 and 2010 to provide direct support to the oversight and administration of the National Industrial Security Program (NISP) and shows actual manning against the planned billets.

Defense Security Service	FY 2009 - Planned	FY 2009 - ACTUAL	FY 2010 - Planned	FY 2010 - ACTUAL
Industrial Security Field Operations (IO)	348	332	388	373
Industrial Security Policy and Programs (IP)	48[1]	38	61	58
Defense Industrial Security Clearance Office (DISCO)	125	107	125	112
DSS Counterintelligence Office (CI)	35	75	87	119
TOTALS	556	552	661	662

IO is an organizational element of DSS that works with cleared companies across the United States to ensure the protection of classified information. IO is comprised of industrial security representatives (ISRs), who are general security specialists, as well as

---

[1] The Biennial Report to Congress on Improving Industrial Security dated September 1, 2009 ("The 2009 Biennial Report"), reflected that 25 billets were authorized for IP during FY 2009. A total of 48 billets were authorized for IP during FY 2009, including 25 Foreign Ownership, Control or Influence (FOCI) personnel.

information systems security professionals (ISSPs), who are technical experts who accredit industry information systems to process classified information. IO also includes a headquarters element that oversees field personnel.

IP is another organizational element of DSS. This office adjudicates Foreign Ownership, Control or Influence (FOCI) issues, administers international programs, and provides industrial and personnel security policy guidance to industry.

DISCO makes determinations regarding the eligibility of contractors and contractor personnel for access to classified information, and processes industrial clearance and personnel security investigative actions. These actions include adjudicating personnel security investigations (PSIs); processing international clearances, overseas assignments, international visit requests, and international transactions relating to personnel and facility clearance verifications; issuing NATO Facility and Personnel Certificates; processing and granting facility clearances (FCLs); monitoring conditions affecting FCLs; and overseeing contractor employees' continued eligibility for access to classified information.

The DSS CI Directorate identifies known or suspected collectors involved in illicit attempts to obtain classified U.S. government information resident in the cleared defense industrial base and articulates the CI threat to industry. The DSS CI Directorate refers incidents indicating possible attempts to steal sensitive technology to national counterintelligence and law enforcement (LE) agencies for investigative follow-up or operational exploitation.

DSS CI specialists work in partnership with industry, other DSS stakeholders, and the LE and intelligence communities (IC) to: determine hostile involvement, refer CI-relevant information reported by cleared industry to the IC and LE, identify intelligence collection trends, and provide a baseline for effective countermeasures to protect U.S. classified information and technologies and programs at risk to foreign or hostile targeting. DSS CI also leverages national CI and Federal LE resources to effectively deter, investigate, neutralize, or exploit penetration attempts, and to provide an aggressive education and awareness program to help industry become the "First Line of Defense" against a pervasive and growing threat. DSS CI encourages the creation of a "culture of catching spies" within the cleared contractor community.

The DSS workforce is in a state of transition with a wide range of experience and expertise. Approximately one-third of the DSS workforce is eligible for retirement, and many of these personnel work in DSS field offices around the country. These employees have extensive knowledge and are well-trained and well-versed in the NISP. The challenge for DSS is effective succession planning to help transition this knowledge base without losing critical skills. DSS also recognizes the challenge of ensuring that new employees are trained and properly resourced to fulfill their missions. In January 2009,

DSS was authorized growth to an end-strength of 1,240 personnel through FY15; however, that growth is on hold, pending a Secretary of Defense-directed revalidation of the analysis that led to the authorization for growth.

All new ISRs assigned at DSS participate in a formal mentoring program with more experienced personnel. This is followed by an intensive four-week Industrial Security Specialist Course, offered in residence at the DSS Academy (DSSA). In addition to the instructors, a number of field personnel and experts within DSS serve as class counselors and provide real-world examples throughout the course. Specialized training in Counterintelligence, Information Systems, Business Structures and other areas is available for individuals serving in those positions.

Field counterintelligence specialists (FCISs) are typically hired into DSS with extensive backgrounds in CI and LE, and have typically served in credentialed CI or federal LE positions within the military services or other U.S. government agencies. Additional training is provided to FCISs and headquarters intelligence analysts via the Joint Counterintelligence Training Academy, or through other IC training sources.

DSS is constantly evaluating its training and assessing the quality of its workforce and is confident it has a high quality, high performing workforce. DSSA undertook the following training initiatives during the reporting period to support the DSS workforce responsible for the oversight of the NISP:

- Conducted a training needs assessment in 2010 based on the results of facilitated focus groups and surveys. Identified skills and competencies that reflect both work and worker-oriented requirements essential to effectively perform the job duties associated with the DSS positions of ISR, FOCI/international specialist and field office chief. Results from the skills analyses and training needs assessment will be used to develop a comprehensive training curriculum and certification program.

- Beta tested a new web-based course, "Understanding Foreign Ownership, Control or Influence (FOCI)." This course will provide a foundational knowledge of the FOCI process and documentation requirements. The target audience for this course includes facility security officers (FSOs) and DoD contractor personnel, DSS industrial security representatives, DoD security specialists, and security specialists from other U.S. Government agencies who interact with NISP cleared companies. This new online course will allow NISP training to be available from any location that provides access to the Internet, thereby eliminating costs of travel and overhead associated with classroom training.

- Launched a new web-based course "Integrating CI and Threat Awareness into your Security Program" in February 2010. This course demonstrates how counterintelligence and threat awareness are essential components of a comprehensive security program. The target audience for this course includes FSOs and DoD contractor personnel, DSS ISRs, DoD security specialists, and other Government security specialists responsible for developing, maintaining, or providing guidance regarding a security program for a unit or facility.

- Launched a new interactive web-based course "Developing a Security and Education Program" in August 2009 which provides an overview of the DoD and NISP policy requirements, best practices and instructional methods for developing and implementing a security education and training program. The target audience for this course includes FSOs and DoD contractor personnel, DSS ISRs, DoD security specialists, and other Government security specialists responsible for developing, maintaining or providing guidance regarding a security education and training program.

During the reporting period, DSS personnel with Industrial Security Program oversight responsibilities participated in and completed 3,240 industrial security training courses. In addition, Industry personnel participated in and completed 20,054 industrial security training courses. Detailed information describing these training courses is contained in Appendix A.

In addition to training that is focused on industrial security, DSS industrial security professionals are participating in the Security Professional Education Development (SPēD) Certification Program. The SPēD Certification Program is a DoD initiative to professionalize the security workforce, ensuring security practitioners can demonstrate proficiency in a common set of competencies. The purpose of the SPēD Certification Program is to promote interoperability, facilitate development and training, and develop a workforce of certified security professionals. Beta-testing of the SPēD program commenced in late FY10.[2]

DoD conducted a thorough study of DSS missions, functions and resources in 2008, which culminated in the Department's decision to strengthen and refocus DSS to meet 21st Century industrial security and counterintelligence needs. As a result, DSS undertook a number of initiatives in the reporting period to improve its oversight of the NISP. These initiatives are outlined in Appendix B.

DSS has established metrics to measure its performance in the oversight and administration of the NISP. The metrics are designed to let DSS know how it is using its resources and to troubleshoot problem areas. To gather this information, DSS has

---

[2] The SPēD program was officially implemented in February 2011.

developed a method of data calls across the agency to collect and compile the information. The following are examples of the metrics, many of which demonstrate significant improvement from similar items highlighted in the 2009 Biennial Report. All information is current as of September 30, 2010. (NOTE: "days" refers to calendar days.)

- Granted 396 interim facility clearance determinations within an average of 47 days.
- Granted 247 final Top Secret facility clearance determinations within an average of 136 days.
- Granted 320 secret and confidential facility clearance determinations within an average of 114 days.
- Completed 80% of scheduled security inspections.
- Average information system accreditation cycle time (33 days). (NOTE: This refers to the time it takes to accredit information systems in cleared facilities to process classified information.)
- Serious security deficiency identification rate for inspections completed during the period October 1, 2008, to September 30, 2010 (7%)[3]. A "serious" security deficiency is substantive in nature and could result in loss or compromise of classified information.
- DSS CI moved from measuring success in terms of activities, e.g., number of briefings and number of suspicious reports received, to measuring the number of known/suspected collectors identified per CI resource. For FY 2010, the goal was to identify 1.5 collectors for every CI full-time employee (FTE); the actual rate of identification was 1.99 collectors per FTE, with 201 known/suspected collectors referred to Federal agencies for investigation or operational activity.

---

[3] The 2009 Biennial Report reflected a 14% serious security deficiency identification rate. This decrease to 7% is a result of expanded field resources allowing greater oversight as well as the augmented ability to address deficiencies before they become serious in nature. This continuing partnership with industry also includes improved training for FSOs.

Topic II: A description of funds authorized, appropriated, or reprogrammed to carry out the requirements of this section, the budget execution of such funds, and the adequacy of budgets provided for performing such purpose.

DoD funded $54.7 million for fiscal year 2009 requirements and $68.5 million for fiscal year 2010 requirements to perform NISP oversight. The FY 2009 and FY 2010 budgets were adequate to perform mission requirements.

DSS Funding for Major Programs
Fiscal Years 2009 and 2010
(in millions of dollars)[4]

	FY09	FY10
NISP[5]	54.7	77.6
CI	12.1	16.9
PSI-I[6]	218.6	218.0
PSC[7]	19.9	26.2
TOTALS	305.3	338.7

---

[4] The 2009 Biennial Report included figures for FY 2009 as of 31 May 2009. The FY 2009 figures provided in this report are actual budget figures as of 30 Septembers 2009. The FY 2010 figures reported in the 2009 Biennial Report were budget estimates for FY 2010. The FY 2010 figures provided in this report are actual budget figures as of 30 September 2010.

[5] NISP funding includes funding for both the Industrial Security Field Operations and Industrial Security Policy and Programs Offices.

[6] PSI-I funding refers to direct reimbursable expenditures to the Office of Personnel Management to conduct investigations for individuals cleared under the National Industrial Security Program. DSS reimburses OPM for these expenses on behalf of the Department of Defense and 23 other Federal Agencies.

[7] PSC funding refers to labor and other operational costs associated with the oversight of the Personnel Security Clearance process as well as the Defense Industrial Security Clearance Office.

Topic III: Statistics on the number of contractors handling classified information of the Department of Defense, and the percentage of such contractors who are subject to foreign ownership, control or influence.

Many of the following statistics highlight significant improvements since the 2009 Biennial Report. All information is current as of September 30, 2010.

- 13,333 facilities cleared under the NISP.

- 702 cleared facilities with a current FOCI mitigation instrument in place. Based on the total cleared population, 5.3% of cleared facilities are cleared under the auspices of a FOCI mitigation agreement.

- 49 companies in various stages of the FOCI mitigation process without current agreements in place. The number of companies in process varies as new cases are opened and resolved. The average number of days to render a decision on the appropriate method of FOCI mitigation is 128 days. This processing time has improved by 47% from 239 days in January 2009.

- During the reporting period, the FOCI case backlog, defined as those cases open for over 120 days, decreased 74% from 88 cases to 23 cases. The 23 backlogged cases are included in the 49 total cases listed above which are not yet mitigated.

- 951,362 active, cleared contractor employees within the NISP.

Topic IV: Statistics on the number of violations identified, enforcement actions taken, and the percentage of such violations occurring at facilities of contractors subject to foreign ownership, control, or influence.

Instances of noncompliance with the National Industrial Security Operating Manual (NISPOM) requirements (hereafter referred to as "deficiencies") found during inspections are categorized as either "serious" or "administrative" deficiencies. Serious deficiencies are substantial deficiencies that could result in loss or compromise of classified information. Examples include process or system failures, such as processing classified information on a non-accredited information system, and transmitting classified information over unsecured lines.

Administrative deficiencies are those conditions that violate a NISPOM requirement but do not directly place classified information at risk of loss or compromise. Some examples include incomplete visitor logs, lack of signatures on briefing statements, and the absence of initials on audit trail review checks. Available data on administrative deficiencies also includes those deficiencies corrected during the conduct of the inspection (i.e., corrected on the spot). All deficiencies noted by DSS during inspections will be reflected in a written report that refers to the applicable paragraph in the NISPOM, NISPOM Supplement, or DoD Overprint to the NISPOM Supplement and include a recommended corrective action. These issuances state detailed requirements for the contractors' industrial security programs and are incorporated by reference into the contracts issued to the cleared companies by U.S. Government agencies.

The most common types of serious deficiencies found during the reporting period were:

- Failure to initiate a preliminary inquiry upon notification of a report of loss, compromise, or suspected compromise of classified information.

- Failure to appropriately mark classified information and material.

- Failure to change safe combinations to closed areas/containers when employees having access were terminated.

- Operating an information system that is processing or will process classified information without appropriate approval.

The chart below reflects data captured by DSS from October 1, 2008, through September 30, 2010.

Summary of DSS Security Inspections of Cleared Facilities
October 1, 2008, to September 30, 2010

Inspection Summary	All Cleared Facilities		Facilities with FOCI Mitigation	
	FY 09	FY10	FY 09	FY10
Security inspections conducted at cleared facilities	8,905	9,442	610	711
Security inspections which identified deficiencies	4,806 (54%)	4,962 (53%)	342 (56%)	371 (52%)
Total security deficiencies identified during inspections*	16,207	18,198	1,073	1,241
Count of administrative deficiencies	14,921	16,698	988	1,151
Count of serious deficiencies	1,286	1,500	85	90
Total enforcement actions taken	82	107	9	12
Marginal security ratings	20	21	3	1
Unsatisfactory security ratings	42	56	6	11
Facility invalidations	20	30	0	0

Note: No system was in place to track deficiencies prior to February 1, 2009. As such, inspection items relating to deficiencies for FY09 are for the time period from February 1, 2009, to September 30, 2009.

BACKGROUND

Once a facility is cleared under the NISP, DSS evaluates the NISP security operations of the organization. At the completion of every security inspection, DSS assigns a security rating. The security ratings are defined as follows:

- The "Superior" security rating is reserved for cleared facilities that have consistently and fully implemented the requirements of the NISPOM in an effective fashion resulting in a security posture of the highest caliber compared with other cleared facilities of similar size and complexity. A cleared facility assigned a rating of "Superior" must have documented and implemented procedures that heighten the security awareness of company employees and must foster a spirit of cooperation within the security community. This rating also requires that a sustained high level of management support must be present for the security program.

- The "Commendable" security rating is assigned to cleared facilities that have fully implemented the requirements of the NISPOM in an effective fashion, resulting in an exemplary security posture compared with other cleared facilities of similar size and complexity. This rating denotes a security program with strong management support, the absence of any serious security issues, and only minor administrative findings.

- The "Satisfactory" security rating is the most common rating and denotes that a cleared facility's security program is in general conformity with the basic requirements of the NISPOM. This rating can be assigned even if there were findings requiring corrective action in one or more of the security program elements within the cleared facility's overall security program. Depending on the circumstances, a satisfactory rating can be assigned even if there were isolated serious findings during the security review.

- The "Marginal" security rating is assigned when a cleared facility's security program is not in general conformity with the basic requirements of the NISPOM. This rating signifies a serious finding in one or more security program areas that could contribute to the eventual compromise of classified information if left uncorrected.

- The "Unsatisfactory" security rating is the most serious negative security rating. An unsatisfactory rating is assigned when circumstances and conditions indicate that the cleared facility has lost, or is in imminent danger of losing, its ability to adequately safeguard the classified information in its possession or to which it has access. This rating is appropriate when the security review results indicate that the cleared facility can no longer credibly demonstrate that it can be depended upon to preclude the disclosure of classified information to unauthorized persons.

DSS conducts a compliance inspection to identify and assess the corrective actions taken by the cleared company at facilities that receive a Marginal or Unsatisfactory security rating. A compliance inspection is viewed by DSS as an enforcement action. The compliance inspection is completed within 120 days after the completion of a security inspection that led to the rating of "Marginal" and 60 calendar days after the completion of a security inspection that led to a rating of "Unsatisfactory."

DSS also has the authority to take the additional enforcement actions of invalidating or revoking a facility clearance. These actions may be taken as a result of a security inspection or compliance inspection, or if DSS becomes aware of information about or actions by the cleared company which adversely affect its ability to protect classified information or its eligibility for a facility clearance. Invalidation of a facility clearance is an interim measure taken by DSS to allow the cleared company to correct the circumstances that negate the integrity of the cleared company's security program.

Invalidation allows the facility to continue to perform on existing classified work with the concurrence of their government contracting activities, but prohibits the facility from bidding on or accepting new work. When invalidating a facility clearance, DSS sets a specific deadline for corrective actions to be taken and follows up to determine whether revalidation or revocation of the facility clearance is necessary.

Revocation of a facility clearance is the most severe enforcement action DSS can take against a facility. Revocation of a facility clearance terminates a cleared company's facility security clearance, rendering it ineligible to perform on classified contracts or access classified information. DSS coordinates revocation decisions with the firm's government contracting activities.

Topic V: An assessment of whether major contractors implementing the program have adequate enforcement programs and have trained their employees adequately in the requirements of the program.

Of the facilities inspected by DSS during the reporting period (October 1, 2008, through September 30, 2010), DSS rated 99.3 % "Satisfactory or better," indicating that the overwhelming majority of facilities cleared under the NISP are effectively protecting classified information. In order to achieve a "Satisfactory" security inspection rating, contractors must have security enforcement and training programs that conform to NISPOM requirements.

DoD does not have a definition as to what constitutes a "major" contractor. Therefore, the data in this report is consolidated for all facilities cleared under the NISP.

A good relationship between DSS and industry depends upon productively balancing cooperation and partnership with strong enforcement and oversight. The DSS workforce is expected to be professional in all dealings with companies, and DSS wants cleared companies to be successful in their security programs.

A company's commitment to implementing the NISP effectively is demonstrated in the establishment and operation of a security program which consistently and fully implements the requirements of the NISP in an effective fashion. Achieving a "Satisfactory" rating or higher requires a sustained high level of management support for the security program. For instance, the following are examples of facility behavior DSS considers in making its determinations about the effectiveness of a company's security program:

- Demonstrated management support and cooperation with the FSO.

- Personal involvement of management in facility security education and awareness programs.

- Absence of any serious security violations that impact integrity of security systems in place.

- Effective security staff who conduct thorough administrative inquiries with prompt reporting, quality investigations, and implementation of appropriate corrective actions when violations are discovered.

To better direct its resources, DSS continues to refine its threat mitigation strategy and methodology to prioritize inspections to better incorporate assessments of counterintelligence threats to cleared U.S. companies. The goal is a coordinated, integrated visit from DSS to the right facility at the right time, with appropriate resources, resulting in a more effective and meaningful inspection.

DSS has established an inspection methodology that applies an evolutionary threat mitigation strategy and methodology to prioritize inspections. This prioritization is based on quantitative risk management factors and serves as the agency's primary assessment of risk as it relates to the overall foreign threat to key technologies within cleared companies. This ensures that the most important or highest risk facilities receive the greatest scrutiny and are expected to have the most stringent security programs.

Topic VI: Trend data on attempts to compromise classified information disclosed to contractors of the Department of Defense to the extent that such data are available.

The DSS CI Directorate produces a family of reports under the "Targeting U.S. Technologies: A Trend Analysis of Reporting from Defense Industry" title. These DSS reports are based on analysis of Suspicious Contact Reports received from cleared companies and identify the most frequently targeted U.S. technologies, reflect the most common collection methods utilized, identify entities attempting the collection, and identify the countries/regions where these collection efforts originate.

The Trends family of products includes a classified and unclassified version of the annual Trends product as well as a classified quarterly Trends product that focuses on a special topic area and relates the threat posed by a specific collection method of operation or the threat posed to a technology sector. Other new product lines are company- and program-based assessments. The company assessments provide a specific cleared company with the threat posed to information and technology resident at its facilities. The program assessments identify the foreign collection threat to a specific defense program.

The most recent unclassified version of the annual Trends report is attached. The classified versions of this report and the quarterly assessments are available upon request.

The unclassified version of the Trends report can also be found on the DSS website at http://dssa.dss.mil/counterintel/2010/DSS_Unclassified.pdf.

"(f) BIENNIAL REPORT.—The Secretary shall report biennially to the congressional defense committees on expenditures and activities of the Department of Defense in carrying out the requirements of this section. The Secretary shall submit the report at or about the same time that the President's budget is submitted pursuant to section 1105(a) of title 31, United States Code, in odd numbered years. The report shall be in an unclassified form (with a classified annex if necessary) and shall cover the activities of the Department of Defense in the preceding two fiscal years, including the following:

"(1) The workforce responsible for carrying out the requirements of this section, including the number and experience of such workforce; training in the performance of industrial security functions; performance metrics; and resulting assessment of overall quality.

"(2) A description of funds authorized, appropriated, or reprogrammed to carry out the requirements of this section, the budget execution of such funds, and the adequacy of budgets provided for performing such purpose.

"(3) Statistics on the number of contractors handling classified information of the Department of Defense, and the percentage of such contractors who are subject to foreign ownership, control, or influence.

"(4) Statistics on the number of violations identified, enforcement actions taken, and the percentage of such violations occurring at facilities of contractors subject to foreign ownership, control, or influence.

"(5) An assessment of whether major contractors implementing the program have adequate enforcement programs and have trained their employees adequately in the requirements of the program.

"(6) Trend data on attempts to compromise classified information disclosed to contractors of the Department of Defense to the extent that such data are available."

APPENDIX A - TRAINING

The following information is provided regarding the quality of training DSS offers.

In December 2008, the Council of Occupational Education (COE) conducted a team visit to DSSA to reaffirm the Academy's national accreditation. The COE is a national accrediting agency that is committed to assuring quality and integrity in career and workforce development. Accreditation is a status granted to an educational institution or program that has been found to meet or exceed stated criteria of educational quality. The purpose of accreditation is to assure the quality of the institution and to assist in the improvement of the institution or program.

The COE team determined that DSSA was in full compliance with all 11 standards of accreditation and the conditions of accreditation. DSSA was granted national re-accreditation by the COE Commission in February 2009. As a result, DSSA is accredited through 2015 and will conduct yearly self-studies mandated and reviewed by the COE. CDSE's initial self-study annual report was submitted and accepted by the COE on November 29, 2010.

DSSA offers 28 online and instructor-led courses related to industrial security functions. The table below provides detailed course and attendance information. During the reporting period, DSS personnel with Industrial Security Program oversight responsibilities participated in and completed 3,240 training courses, and industry personnel participated in and completed 20,054 training courses.

Industrial Security Course Participants
October 1, 2008, to September 30, 2010

Course	Description	DSS Attendees	Industry Attendees
FSO Role in the NISP	Describes the role of the FSO in the NISP	375	3907
Getting Started Seminar for New FSOs	Provides new FSOs with an opportunity to apply fundamental NISP requirements	19	335
Essentials of Industrial Security Management	Covers basic NISP requirements with emphasis on cleared contractor responsibilities	286	2530

Protecting Secret and Confidential Documents	Focuses on NISP requirements for cleared contractor facilities with authorization to store classified information	104	955
Introduction to Industrial Security	Provides an introduction to the DoD Industrial Security Program	158	485
Introduction to Physical Security	Provides students with a basic understanding of the theories and principles involved in the application of physical security in the protection of DoD assets	137	451
Visits and Meetings in the NISP	Covers the rules and procedures for classified visits and meetings for cleared companies participating in the NISP	141	528
ISFD online course	Provides step-by-step instructions on the use of the Industrial Security Facilities Database (ISFD)	140	340
ISFD for DSS users online course	Provides step-by-step instructions on the use of the ISFD	177	21
JPAS/JCAVS Training for Security Professionals	Provides an overview of the Joint Personnel Adjudication System (JPAS) and a detailed explanation of its subsystem, the Joint Clearance and Access Verification System (JCAVS) used by DoD personnel security managers and FSOs for eligibility and investigation verification	32	362
JPAS/JCAVS Virtual Training online course	Provides an overview of JPAS and a detailed explanation of its subsystem, JCAVS, which are used extensively by DoD personnel security managers and FSOs for eligibility and investigation verification	76	545
Safeguarding Classified Information in the NISP	Covers the rules and procedures for protecting classified information and material in the NISP	19	1388
Derivative Classification	Explains how to derivatively classify national security information from a classification management perspective	146	1301

Transmission and Transportation for Industry	Examines the requirements and methods for transmitting or transporting classified information and other classified material in accordance with NISP	144	891
Marking Classified Information	Examines the requirements and methods for marking classified documents and other classified material	218	1476
Security Awareness For Educators (SAFE)	Addresses how to create an effective security awareness and education program and identifies solutions for overcoming the various challenges surrounding this responsibility	19	91
SAP Orientation	Introduces students to DoD Special Access Programs (SAPs)	40	300
NISPOM Chapter 8 Security Requirements	Introduces the security requirements for safeguarding classified information processed and stored in information systems at cleared company facilities	142	994
NISPOM Chapter 8 Security Implementation	Teaches the basics of security for Local Area Networks and practices implementation of the security requirements described in Chapter 8 of the NISPOM	19	227
Information System Security Basics	Introduces the basics of information system security	148	1,514
Business Structures in the NISP	Covers the most common business structures ISRs encounter when processing a company for a facility clearance	238	303
Industrial Security Mentoring Program	Introduces new DSS ISRs to the Industrial Security Program	29	N/A
Industrial Security Specialist Course	Trains new DSS ISRs to perform basic responsibilities, including initial clearance and recurring inspections of non-complex cleared facilities approved to store classified material under the NISP	56	N/A

Fundamentals of Industrial Security Level 1	Provides the fundamental knowledge of the NISP	64	N/A
Fundamentals of Industrial Security Level 2	Builds upon the knowledge and skills learned in the Fundamentals of Industrial Security Level 1 course and trains the ISR to perform inspections of non-complex possessing facilities that are approved to store classified material under NISP	43	N/A
Introduction to Information Security	Provides a basic understanding of the legal and regulatory basis for the DoD Information Security program	126	466
Developing a Security Education Program	Provides a thorough overview of the DoD and NISP policy requirements, best practices, and instructional methods for developing and implementing a security education program	100	340
Integrating CI and Threat	Provides thorough overview of CI and threat awareness, essential components of a comprehensive security program	44	304

APPENDIX B - OVERALL PROGRAM ACCOMPLISHMENTS

During fiscal year 2008, the Secretary of Defense directed, and the Under Secretary of Defense for Intelligence convened, an outside panel of experts to examine the four mission areas of DSS (industrial security, education and training, personnel security clearances, and information technology). As a result of this study, DoD initiated steps to strengthen and refocus DSS to meet 21st Century industrial security and CI needs. Toward this end, DSS will enhance its oversight under the NISP to include an increased focus on CI and security education. During the reporting period, DSS has:

- Completed a reorganization of the DSS Headquarters Industrial Security Program. The new organization allows for increased emphasis and support to the Headquarters, Field and Counterintelligence missions and enhances transparency at the senior management level.

- Completed a reorganization of the DSS field structure to ensure integration of Counterintelligence, Information Technology Security, and Industrial Security generalists at both the regional and Headquarters level.

- Launched the second annual Voice of Industry Survey in order to reach out to industry partners.[8] The survey covered areas in which DSS interacts with industry, and feedback is used to address customer service issues and identify areas where improvements may be necessary. Responses were overwhelmingly positive.

- Launched the Partnership with Industry Program, a professional development exchange program between DSS industrial security representatives and industry's facility security officers.

- Developed a new matrix to improve consistency in how DSS assigns facility ratings. By developing a numerical rating matrix, the intent is to produce maximum consistency across the DSS areas of operation and reduce subjectivity to a minimum.

- Instituted an Industrial Security Field Operations Quality Assurance Office (QAO). This office is tasked to assess field processes and procedures, identify inconsistencies or issues, and enhance policy, training, or management support as needed to mitigate any shortcomings. Additionally, this office identifies best practices and ensures these are shared with personnel nationwide. A major effort of the QAO was to conduct Staff Assessment Visits of all 26 field offices. These visits used a standard process to provide a DSS-wide operations analysis and

---

[8] The first annual Voice of Industry Survey was conducted from December 2008 to February 2009.

identify best practices and areas that may require process improvements or guidance revision.

- Created inspection plans specifically for facilities under FOCI mitigation agreements or those that are freight forwarders for classified information. By tailoring inspections for the unique considerations of these types of facilities, DSS is working to ensure even more effective protection of classified information entrusted to industry.

- During June 2008, DSS established a DISCO advance office in Linthicum, Maryland, to help address a 2005 Base Realignment and Closure Act recommendation to co-locate all DoD adjudication capabilities at Fort Meade by September 15, 2011. In anticipation of the 400-mile relocation of DISCO from Columbus, Ohio, DSS also authorized the use of over-hire authorizations so new employees could be hired in advance of the departure of existing employees who were not transferring. By September 30, 2010, 34 percent of the DISCO workforce was in place in Maryland.

- For FY10, DSS met Intelligence Reform and Terrorism Prevention Act (IRTPA) personnel clearance adjudication timelines for the 113,256 cases that fell under DSS cognizance. The IRTPA requires 90% of initial adjudication determinations to be made in an average of 20 days. IRTPA requires 90% of reinvestigation determinations to be made in an average of 30 days.

- Established a Facilities of Interest List (FIL) that defines a risk-based approach to supporting inspections and allows the agency to move from a subjective approach to one that is proactive, integrated, and objective. DSS uses the FIL to determine the risk to a facility, to prioritize its workload based on the risk, and to tailor inspections to address the risk.

- Established DSS cross-regional inspection teams for complex cleared facilities. This approach aids the professional development of the DSS workforce by exposing personnel to facilities and personnel with whom they would not necessarily have the opportunity to work in their own geographic regions.

- Created a senior FOCI oversight manager position to improve oversight of cleared companies under FOCI mitigation.

- Established enhanced oversight and inspection process for firms under FOCI.

- Developed more robust FOCI analytical capabilities. As a result, DSS now has improved oversight of its FOCI facilities, reviews all facility clearance packages to ensure proper reporting of FOCI, and performs financial analyses to clarify complex financial arrangements shielding foreign investments.

- Increased the number of FOCI action officers at DSS Headquarters.

- Created two FOCI Divisions:

  - FOCI Analytic Division: Responsible for ensuring that available data is analyzed and applied when determining whether a company is under FOCI and in deciding which risk mitigation measure is acceptable.

  - FOCI Operations Division: Responsible for the implementation of FOCI mitigation plans.

- Launched the Electronic Facility Clearance (e-FCL) System, a web-based application developed for the collection of required company forms and documentation necessary for facility clearance and FOCI mitigation processing.

- Established a financial analysis capability to identify and monitor business ownership structures of NISP contractors for potential indirect foreign control or influence.

- Moved from classroom-based training to more web-based training. This allows DSSA to deliver training to those who need it, when and where they need it.

- Increased the number of course offerings available at DSSA and developed new training products and services.

- In FY10, the DSS CI Directorate identified 201 known/suspected illegal collectors and referred these cases to Federal action agencies.[9]

- Fostered stronger relationships with Federal law enforcement and intelligence action agencies; embedded a senior liaison officer at FBI and ICE headquarters and embedded cyber liaison officers at the National Cyber Investigative Joint Task Force, U.S. Cyber Command, and the Defense Cyber Crime Center.

---

[9] In this context, "Federal action agencies" refers to USG agencies with law enforcement or other operational/National Security authorities to take actions against the referrals transmitted by DSS, including FBI and DHS/Immigration and Customs Enforcement (ICE), and any agency with Title 18 law enforcement or Title 50 National Security authorities.

- Expanded the CI analytical product line beyond the annual Trends documents to include a classified quarterly Trends product that focuses on a special topic area and relates the threat posed by a specific collection method of operation, or the threat posed to a technology sector. Other new product lines include company- and program-based assessments. The company assessments provide a specific cleared company with the threat posed to information and technology resident at its facilities. The program assessments identify the foreign collection threat to a specific defense program.

- Created the DSS Award for Excellence in Counterintelligence to recognize annually the cleared contractors who best demonstrate the ability to stop foreign theft of U.S. defense technology.

- Created the DSS Operations and Analysis Group to identify threats and internal and external DSS vulnerabilities, and to facilitate exchange of security and CI-related information within DSS components.

- Increased the number of CI personnel at headquarters and in the field.